USBORNE UNDERSTANDING SCIENCE

ELECTRICITY AND MAGNETISM

Peter Adamczyk and Paul-Francis Law

Designed by
Stephen Wright

Edited by
Jane Chisholm and **Eliot Humberstone**

Illustrated by
Andy Burton

Additional illustrations by
Dan Courtney and **Chris Shields**

Additional designs by
Linda Penny

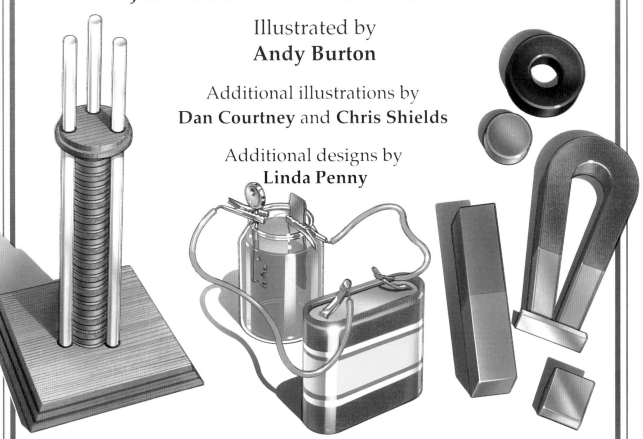

Contents

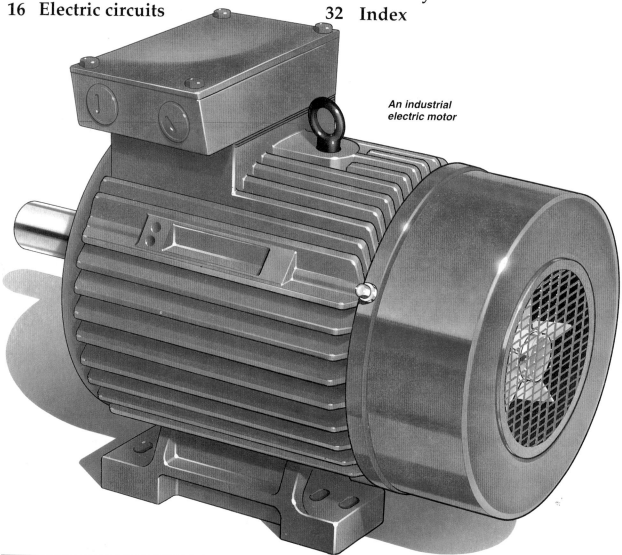

An industrial electric motor

First published in 1993 by Usborne Publishing Ltd,
83-85 Saffron Hill, London EC1N 8RT, England.
Universal edition.
Copyright 1993 Usborne Publishing Ltd.
The name Usborne and the device are Trade Marks of
Usborne Publishing Ltd.
UE First published in America March 1994

537
ADA

Introducing electricity and magnetism

Electricity plays such an important part in our lives that it's something most of us take for granted. At the flick of a switch a light comes on or a picture appears on a television set. In hot countries, people depend on it to run fans, refrigerators and cooling systems. In cooler countries, electricity provides light and warmth for houses, offices and factories. But what is it and how does it work?

Television set

Electricity may be described as an example of energy, which can be easily transferred to and from other forms, such as heat and light. The electricity we use is called current electricity. Most of it is produced, or generated, in power stations, but some of it also comes from electrical cells and batteries.

A power station

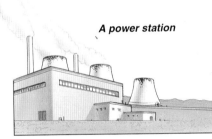

But current electricity is not the only kind. You can find examples of natural electricity all around you - even in your body. Lightning is a type of electricity, and so are the crackles that sometimes come from pulling a sweater over your head. This kind of electricity is called static. You can find out more about it on pages 6-9.

Lightning striking a power cable

People have known about the effects of static electricity since ancient times. But it was only in the last century that scientists discovered how to generate current electricity. There have been amazing developments since then, and it is now possible to generate electricity using energy from many different sources. For example, in some parts of the world, it is generated by heat from hot rocks deep inside the earth. This is called geothermal energy.

A geothermal power station

The mysterious properties of magnets were first observed by the Ancient Greeks over 2000 years ago. But it is only relatively recently that scientists have begun to investigate magnetism and what lies behind it. A magnet is something (usually metal) that can attract similar metals, making them stick to it. Magnets also form the basis for compasses used in navigation. This is because a bar-shaped magnet suspended in water or air will always rotate until it is pointing in a north-south direction.

A marine compass

Soon after the invention of the first battery, scientists began to wonder whether electricity and magnetism might not be related in some way. In the 19th century, the English scientist Michael Faraday showed how a moving magnet could create an electric current. Soon after that came the startling discovery that electricity could be used to create magnetism. With this developed a new branch of science, known as electromagnetism, which lies at the heart of many of the machines we use today - from tape recorders to electric motors.

An electromagnetic crane

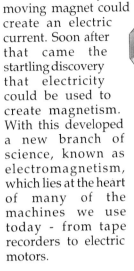

In less than 200 years, people have discovered how to harness and use electricity in many different ways. With new ideas being developed and tested all the time, the next 200 years are likely to be just as exciting.

Words in italic type

Some words in the text appear in italic type with a small star (like this: *friction**). You can find definitions of these words, as well as most common words connected with electricity, in the glossary on page 31.

Electrical energy

Electricity is an example of energy, and energy is what makes things move or change. Other forms of energy include heat, light, mechanical, nuclear, chemical and kinetic energy (the energy of moving things). Whenever something moves or changes in any way, it happens because energy is being transferred from one form to another.

Most of the electricity we use is generated in power stations by burning fuels, such as coal and oil. Fuels contain chemical energy, which is transferred to electrical energy in the process. Some power stations use nuclear fuel, which makes use of the enormous energy available when unstable *atoms** are broken apart. Another source of electricity comes from *electrical cells** and batteries, which also contain chemical energy.

A 9V battery

Energy efficiency

Ordinary light bulbs (known as incandescent bulbs) are actually very inefficient. Most of the energy they transfer is in the form of unwanted heat. As little as 10% is light.

But you don't have to waste all this electrical energy. You can buy bulbs that transfer most of it into light, rather than heat. These kinds of bulbs are called fluorescent. They produce just as much brightness, but using much less energy. The latest compact models can save as much as 80% of the energy used by an incandescent bulb. Although they are more expensive, they last much longer.

Compact fluorescent bulb

Where energy comes from

Scientists think of energy as changing from one form to another, rather then being created or destroyed.

One of the most important sources of energy on Earth is the light and heat from the Sun, which is called solar energy. Plants are able to transfer light energy into food (chemical energy) to store and feed themselves. Some of this is then passed on to the animals who eat the plants.

Most of the electricity we use comes from coal, oil and gas. These are known as fossil fuels, because they have taken millions of years to develop. Coal comes from the remains of dead plants; oil and gas from the remains of tiny sea creatures (such as microscopic algae).

This picture shows how the energy on Earth is constantly being transferred from one form to another.

Measuring energy

Energy is measured in units called joules (J). One joule is the energy needed to raise the temperature of one kilogram of water by 1°C. The rate at which a device transfers energy from one form to another is known as its power. Power is measured in watts (W). 1W means that 1J is transferred every second.

A 100W bulb transfers more energy per second than a 60W bulb, and produces a brighter light.

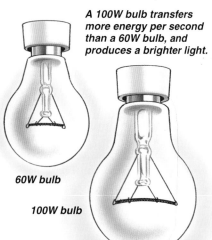

60W bulb

100W bulb

Did you know?

Many of the measurements used in electricity are named after scientists who made important contributions to the subject.

The *watt* gets its name from James Watt (1736 -1819), the Scottish engineer who invented the first efficient steam engine.

Watt's engine

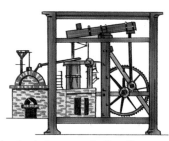

The *joule* is named after the English physicist James Joule (1818 -1889). He studied energy transfer and the link between electricity and heat.

Electricity is transported to homes, offices and factories by means of cables. These are buried underground or carried by huge metal structures called pylons.

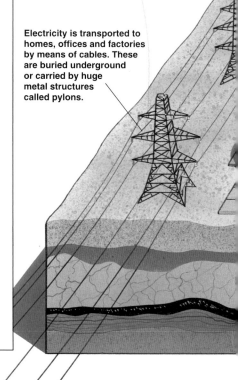

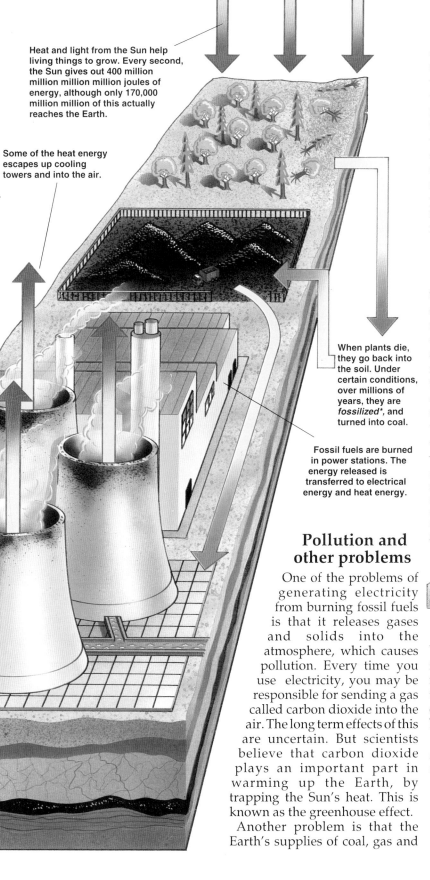

Heat and light from the Sun help living things to grow. Every second, the Sun gives out 400 million million million million joules of energy, although only 170,000 million million of this actually reaches the Earth.

Some of the heat energy escapes up cooling towers and into the air.

When plants die, they go back into the soil. Under certain conditions, over millions of years, they are *fossilized**, and turned into coal.

Fossil fuels are burned in power stations. The energy released is transferred to electrical energy and heat energy.

oil are limited. Once these are used up, they would take many millions of years to replace, even with the right conditions. This is one reason why some modern power stations now use nuclear fuel instead.

Carbon dioxide   Sun's rays

This diagram shows how carbon dioxide traps the Sun's rays.

Alternative energy sources

Scientists are also exploring alternative, "renewable", sources of energy. These include harnessing energy from wind, waves, and water, and using geothermal energy (heat from inside the Earth). Some of these methods involve the development of technology, such as windmills and water wheels, used by earlier civilizations.

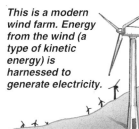

This is a modern wind farm. Energy from the wind (a type of kinetic energy) is harnessed to generate electricity.

Pollution and other problems

One of the problems of generating electricity from burning fossil fuels is that it releases gases and solids into the atmosphere, which causes pollution. Every time you use electricity, you may be responsible for sending a gas called carbon dioxide into the air. The long term effects of this are uncertain. But scientists believe that carbon dioxide plays an important part in warming up the Earth, by trapping the Sun's heat. This is known as the greenhouse effect.

Another problem is that the Earth's supplies of coal, gas and

Muscle power

You can even generate electricity from your own muscles. When you ride a bicycle with a dynamo, you transfer energy into enough electricity to work the bicycle lights.

Bicycle dynamo fitted to wheel

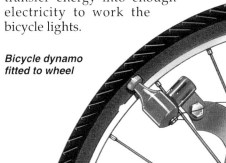

Static electricity

It's possible to stick an inflated balloon to the wall without using tape or glue - just electricity. The type of electricity involved is called electrostatics, or static electricity.

But first you have to rub the balloon against your hair or a woolly sweater for a minute or two. This causes electric charges to pass to the surface of the balloon, giving the balloon extra electric charges.

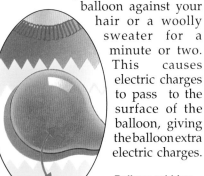

Balloon rubbing against sweater

If you hold the balloon against the wall, the extra charges are attracted to opposite charges on the wall. This is what makes the balloon stick. The longer you charge it (by rubbing), the longer it will stick. Eventually the charges will be *neutralized** and the balloon will fall.

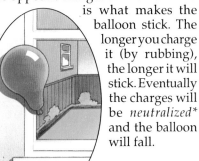

Balloon sticking to wall

Just as substances with opposite charges attract each other, those with the same charge push away from one another. You can see this if you give two balloons the same charge. Charge one and tie it to the back of a chair. Charge the other in the same way and hold it near the first. The first balloon will bob away to avoid it.

Balloons repelling each other

Discovering static

Static was first observed over 2000 years ago in Ancient Greece. People who wore brooches made from amber (a golden fossilized sap from trees) sometimes noticed a tingling feeling if the amber rubbed against their clothes. On a dry day, it might even crackle when pulled away from the material. Many words connected with electricity come from the Greek word for amber: *electron.*

If amber is rubbed with a dry cloth, it can attract lightweight things, such as leaves and feathers.

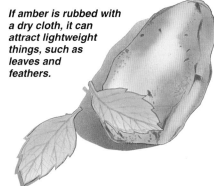

Where can you find static?

You can find examples of static all around you. On a cold, dry day when you've been exercising , the action of your arms and legs causes your clothes to rub together, and this may generate a static charge. It's even possible to get a slight shock if you touch something metal after running or walking briskly. This won't happen if it's wet or damp, because the static is discharged due to the moisture in air. Certain materials combined, such as wool, nylon, fur and hair, generate static more easily than others. If you pull a sweater over your head on a dry night, you might hear crackling. If the lights are turned off, you might even see a spark.

Testing for static charges

Using a few household objects, you can test how easy it is for a material to become statically charged. Turn on a tap to get a very thin flow of water. Rub a plastic ruler up and down against your sweater a few times, then move it towards the flow. The water should bend towards the ruler. See if you can get a similar result with other things, such as a wooden spoon and a coin.

WARNING: Never try water-bending experiments with electricity from the mains. It is extremely dangerous. Always keep appliances away from water.

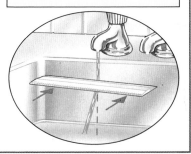

Super static charges

Using friction, a Van de Graaff generator can build such a high static charge that it makes your hair stand on end. It consists of a rubber belt, which rubs continuously against two rollers. This action transfers energetic charges to the outside of a metal dome. If you touch the dome, the charges are shared with the outside of your body and hair. As all the hairs have the same charge, each one tries to get as far from the others as possible.

Van de Graaff generator

Dome

How does static work?

All materials are made of positive and negative electrical charges. But most of the time we are unaware of them because they cancel each other out. In order to stay balanced, substances with a surplus of opposite charges will attract one another. The attraction may even be strong enough to make them stick together.

Under certain conditions, negative electrical charges build up on the surface of an object. The charges remain "static" (or still) until they find some way to escape, or be discharged. When this happens, their energy is transferred to other forms. If this happens quickly, it produces a spark.

Scientists use diagrams of atoms, called models, to help show the different parts, but atoms don't actually look like them. An atom is mostly made up of empty space. The distance between the units is enormous compared to the scale of the atom, so it would be impossible to show the correct scale.

This atomic model, known as the cloud or petal model, is one of the most up-to-date.

Electrons spin around the nucleus in different energy levels. There is an electron moving somewhere in each of these "petals" or "clouds".

At the heart of the atom is a nucleus, which contains units called protons and neutrons.

This atomic model, known as Bohr's model, is often found in older school textbooks.

Nucleus

Electrons

Some atoms bind their electrons strongly, while others bind them weakly. When two substances of different binding strengths are rubbed together, the electrons are drawn to the stronger one. The substance that loses electrons becomes positively charged and the one that gains electrons becomes negatively charged. These "unbalanced" atoms are called positive and negative ions.

A positive ion (an atom with more protons than electrons)

A negative ion (an atom with more electrons than protons)

What are electrical charges?

The structure of atoms (the tiny units that make up everything) is often used to explain electrical charges. Each atom is made up of a number of even smaller units, which have an electrical charge: electrons (negative), protons (positive) and neutrons (neutral). Atoms of different substances have different numbers of protons, but each atom has an equal number of protons and electrons. This is what keeps it balanced.

Most of the atom is just empty space. What holds it together is the attraction between the protons and electrons.

Did you know?

Detectives use static to identify invisible fingerprints left on plastic or paper surfaces. A metal plate coated with a fine dark powder is given a high positive static charge. When the specimen comes into contact with the positively charged powder, it receives a negative charge. The powder is attracted to it, and sticks to the tacky ridges of the fingerprint. Photocopiers work in a similar way. Dark powder, called toner, is attracted to charged parts of a metal plate. The image is then transferred to paper.

Thunder and lightning

Lightning is really a giant spark of static, which heats the air, producing a flash of light. The air expands suddenly, emitting a shock wave which we hear as thunder. A lightning bolt carries so much energy that it can destroy buildings and kill people. But it cannot be used as a source of power. No one knows where it will strike next, and when it does strike, too much energy is available too fast for it to be stored and used.

What causes lightning?

A thundercloud contains billions of water droplets and ice crystals. It is thought that static builds up when these crash into each other. As they do so, they exchange some of their charges. The larger drops gain a negative charge and fall to the bottom of the cloud, repelling negative charges on the buildings below. This induces a concentration of positive charges there.

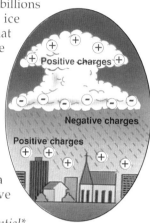

A negative electric *potential** now exists between the cloud and the earth. This would drive the cloud's charges toward the earth, except that the air between them is a strong *insulator**. But the insulation is broken if an enormous charge builds up. When this happens, the charge at the base of the cloud discharges itself by seeking a path to the ground with flashes called leader strokes.

As one of these leader strokes gets close, a large positive charge called a streamer stroke builds up on the ground. It rises until it meets the leader stroke 10-20m (30-60ft) above the ground. These strokes create a "channel", along which a second, much more powerful, flash can run. This is called a return stroke.

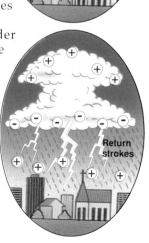

In a thunderstorm, air moving in a thundercloud transfers solar energy to electrical energy. During a lightning strike this is immediately transferred to heat, light and sound.

A lightning bolt is made up of three or four strokes, separated by gaps of a few millionths of a second. This is why it appears to flicker.

During a storm, some objects can become highly charged. This *ionizes** the air around them, causing a bluish glow. This is called St Elmo's fire and it is seen most often on the masts of ships at sea.

You are safe inside a car, as long as you don't touch the sides. This is because static charges collect on the outsides of objects.

If a tall tree or building is unprotected by a lightning conductor, it may get struck.

Some tall buildings have devices called lightning conductors on them. They keep the lightning away from the building.

How conductors work

A lightning conductor is a thick copper strip running down the side of a building. It connects sharp metal points on the roof to a large metal plate in the ground below. Electric charges tend to concentrate around the most sharply curved parts of a conductor, such as the points. Charges in the air are attracted to opposite charges on the points, and similar charges are repelled. This is known as point action.

Diagram showing how a lightning conductor works

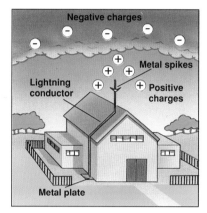

A conductor uses point action to neutralize the charge in nearby thunderclouds. Negative charges on the conductor are repelled by the cloud and move down the conductor into the ground. This leaves a concentration of positive charges at the top. These positive charges spray away from the spikes, neutralizing the negative charge on the cloud directly above the building. So conductors should really be called "neutralizers", as they help to prevent lightning from forming, rather than protecting when it does strike.

Make your own conductor

To see how a metal point can neutralize a static charge, you could repeat the experiment for bending water on page 6. Charge up a plastic ruler and bend the water. Get a friend to move a pin or needle slowly toward the ruler. The sharp point makes it easy for positive charges to escape and neutralize the negative charge on the ruler. When this happens, the water stops bending.

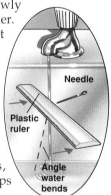

Did you know?

There are many types of natural electricity, not just lightning. Messages are passed along the nerves of our bodies by small electrical impulses, and our hearts beat due to electrical signals. Some creatures use electricity generated in their bodies to navigate, to attack and for protection. The electric ray can produce a current big enough to kill a large fish.

Electric ray, also known as a Pisces ray

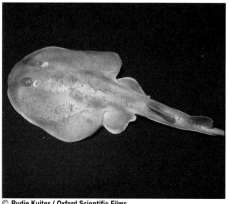

© Rudie Kuiter / Oxford Scientific Films

Magnetism

Magnetism gets its name from Magnesia in Turkey where, over 2000 years ago, the Ancient Greeks came across pieces of rock which possessed mysterious powers. They found that it could attract metals, making them stick together. The rock was a form of iron ore which we now call magnetite.

A magnet is the name for a substance (usually a metal, such as iron or steel) that has been "magnetized" so that it will behave like magnetite. Any metal that can do this is described as magnetic.

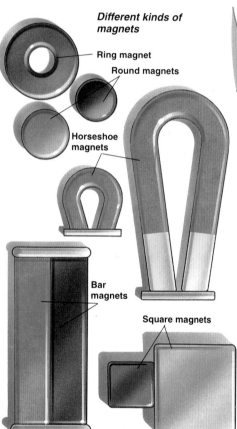

Different kinds of magnets

Ring magnet

Round magnets

Horseshoe magnets

Bar magnets

Square magnets

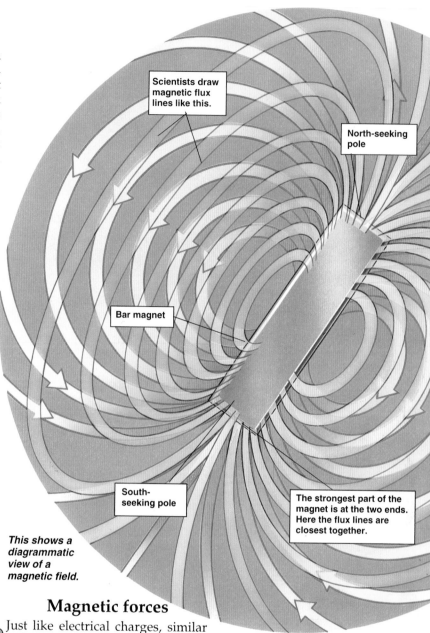

Scientists draw magnetic flux lines like this.

North-seeking pole

Bar magnet

South-seeking pole

The strongest part of the magnet is at the two ends. Here the flux lines are closest together.

This shows a diagrammatic view of a magnetic field.

Magnetic forces

Just like electrical charges, similar poles repel each other, and opposite poles attract. You can feel the force of attraction if you move two opposite poles apart. If you hold similar poles together, the magnets will push away from each other.

Another characteristic of a magnet is that if it is left to float in water, or suspended in air from a thread tied exactly around its middle, it will always end up pointing in a north-south direction. The two ends of a magnet are described as north-seeking and south-seeking poles.

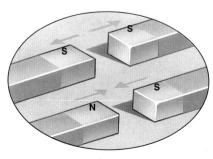

Magnetic fields

Magnetic objects entering the area around a magnet are affected by the magnet's forces of attraction and repulsion. This area is called a magnetic field. The stronger the magnet, the larger the field. If you divide a magnet in half, it produces two whole fields (not two halves of one field). Although the field itself is invisible, there are ways of finding out what it looks like.

Take a strong bar magnet, a sheet of stiff white paper or thin cardboard and some iron filings. Sprinkle the iron filings evenly over the paper, and hold it tightly about 3-6cm (1.5-2.5 inches) above the magnet on a table. Then slowly move the paper down towards the table.

The iron filings will quickly move and settle into a symmetrical pattern created by the force of the magnet. The pattern shows the lines of force, called field lines, or flux lines. The field is strongest where the flux lines are closest together. Tap the paper gently to help the filings settle in the weaker parts of the field.

Magnetic flux lines shown with iron filings

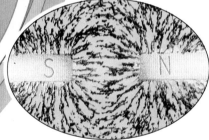

© Richard Megna / Fundamental / Science Photo Library

Creating a magnet

Metal objects that are attracted by magnets become magnetic too, although this effect often dies away once the object has been removed from the magnetic field.

You can create a magnet yourself by magnetizing something metal (such as a needle or a paper clip). Stroke it with a strong magnet, in the same direction, about 30 or 40 times.

Magnetizing a needle

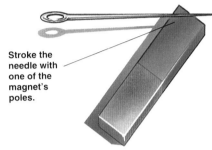

Stroke the needle with one of the magnet's poles.

Some metals, such as pure iron, can be magnetized very easily, but they lose their magnetism quickly too. Steel, on the other hand, takes longer to magnetize, but keeps its magnetism for longer. To see the difference, try magnetizing an iron nail and a steel needle.

Something that behaves like a magnet after it has been removed from the field of the inducing magnet is said to have "residual", or "induced", magnetism.

Testing magnetic power

Using a magnet, try to pick up a chain of pins or paper clips, each one clinging to the one above. The stronger the magnetic field, the longer the chain will be. The power of attraction is strongest closest to the magnet. So if you remove a pin close to the magnet, the rest of the chain will collapse. But if you remove the magnet itself, some of the pins may have enough residual magnetism to attract each other.

Magnetized paper clips

Explaining magnetism

For centuries, people have puzzled over what causes magnetism. Scientists now believe that magnets are made up of millions of tiny units, grouped together in clusters called domains.

Each unit acts like a miniature magnet. In ordinary metals these domains are all jumbled up, so their magnetic fields cancel each other out. But when a metal is put close enough to a magnet to be affected by its magnetic field, the domains all line up in the same direction and the metal is magnetized.

Jumbled domains

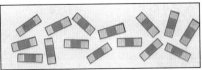

Ordered domains

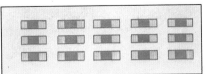

Looking at magnetic fields

You can see a different cross-section of the same magnetic field by repeating the experiment above, but with two sets of paper and iron filings. Move the second piece of paper down until it is 2-3cm (1 inch) above the first, and then sprinkle it with iron filings. A slightly different pattern should appear.

1st cross-section of field lines

2nd cross-section of field lines

Bar magnet

Magnetic compasses

The earliest use of a magnet was probably as a compass needle. Records show Chinese sailors using compasses for navigation, as much as a thousand years ago. Compasses allowed them to steer a course without the aid of a landmark, or even the Sun or stars.

The first scientific attempts to explain how this worked suggested that the compass needle was "attracted" to certain stars. People noticed that when a compass needle came into contact with a larger magnet, it would align itself with it (opposite poles together). In 1600, the English scientist William Gilbert put forward a revolutionary new idea to explain how a compass worked. He suggested that the Earth itself might be a giant magnet.

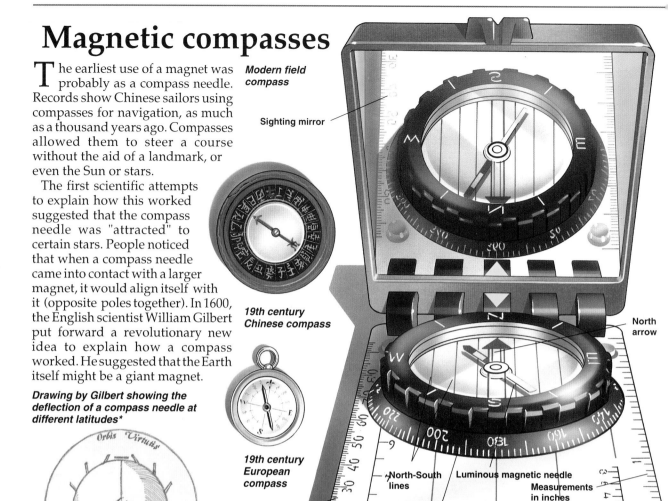

Modern field compass

Sighting mirror

19th century Chinese compass

19th century European compass

Drawing by Gilbert showing the deflection of a compass needle at different latitudes*

Orbis Virtutis

Axis

North arrow

North-South lines

Luminous magnetic needle

Measurements in inches

Graduation scale

Metric measurements

Make your own compass

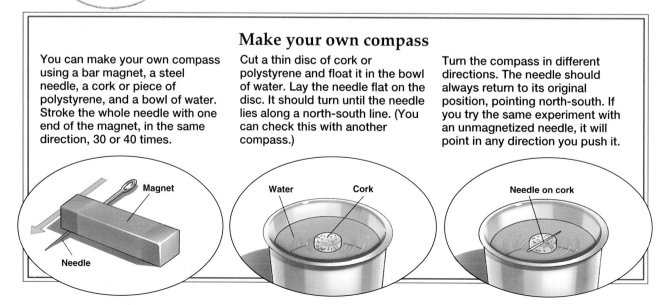

You can make your own compass using a bar magnet, a steel needle, a cork or piece of polystyrene, and a bowl of water. Stroke the whole needle with one end of the magnet, in the same direction, 30 or 40 times.

Cut a thin disc of cork or polystyrene and float it in the bowl of water. Lay the needle flat on the disc. It should turn until the needle lies along a north-south line. (You can check this with another compass.)

Turn the compass in different directions. The needle should always return to its original position, pointing north-south. If you try the same experiment with an unmagnetized needle, it will point in any direction you push it.

Magnet

Needle

Water

Cork

Needle on cork

The Earth as a magnet

We now know that Gilbert was right, except in one important detail. The magnetic poles of the Earth are not in exactly the same position as the geographical poles (what we call North and South Pole). In fact the magnetic poles wander about very slowly. At the moment, magnetic north pole is at Prince of Wales island in northern Canada. The difference between magnetic north (which compasses point towards) and geographical north (sometimes called "true north") is called the angle of declination. This angle varies from place to place around the world.

The flux lines of the Earth's magnetic field curve between the magnetic poles. They do not follow the Earth's surface, but enter and leave the ground at different angles in different places. The angle at which they do this is known as the angle of dip.

If you hang a bar magnet with a thread exactly around its middle, you may notice that one end of it dips down slightly. In the northern hemisphere, it is the north-seeking pole of a magnet or compass that dips down. Below the equator, it is the south-seeking pole.

Pole dipping down slightly

Diagram showing the Earth as a giant bar magnet

Geographical North Pole

Magnetic north pole

Magnetic field lines

The Earth tilts on its axis at a 23½° angle.

Geographical South Pole

Magnetic south pole

Animal compasses

Each year, millions of birds fly great distances between their winter and summer quarters. Without the help of landmarks or the Sun and stars, they follow a similar route through skies that are often dark and cloudy. Scientists believe that the birds may find their way by sensing the Earth's magnetic field, and that this may also apply to other sea animals, such as whales. It is not clear how they do this, but it may have something to do with tiny grains of magnetite that have been found in the bodies of certain creatures, including bees and butterflies.

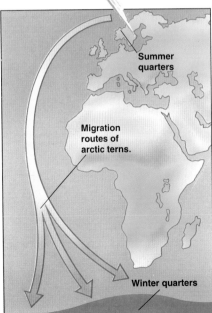

Every year, birds like this arctic tern fly to the Antarctic and back from breeding sites in the Arctic.

Summer quarters

Migration routes of arctic terns.

Winter quarters

Cells and batteries

One of the most convenient ways of obtaining electricity is from a cell or battery. The electrical energy they provide comes from a chemical reaction between the different substances inside them. When only one pair of substances is used, we call it a cell. Batteries are made up of a number of cells linked together.

Did you know?

Three years before Volta built his battery, the Italian scientist Luigi Galvani (1737-98) discovered that the leg of a dead frog twitched when touched with two different metals. Galvani called this effect "animal electricity", thinking that the electrical energy had come from the animal. But Volta showed that this was not the case. What had actually happened was that the body fluids had acted as an *electrolyte** between the two metals, creating a simple cell.

G
F
D
M
D
C
C

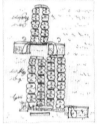

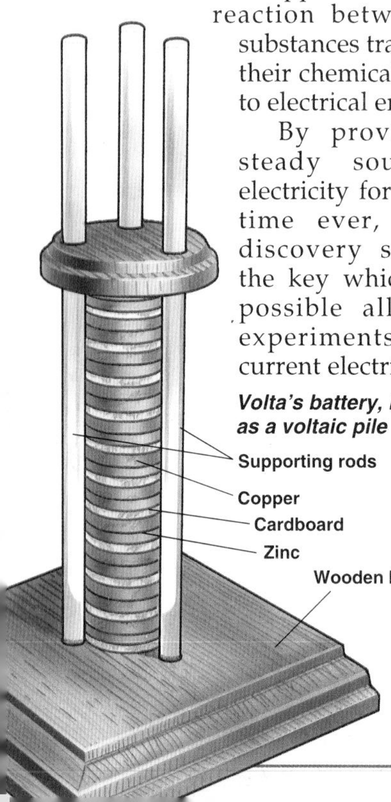

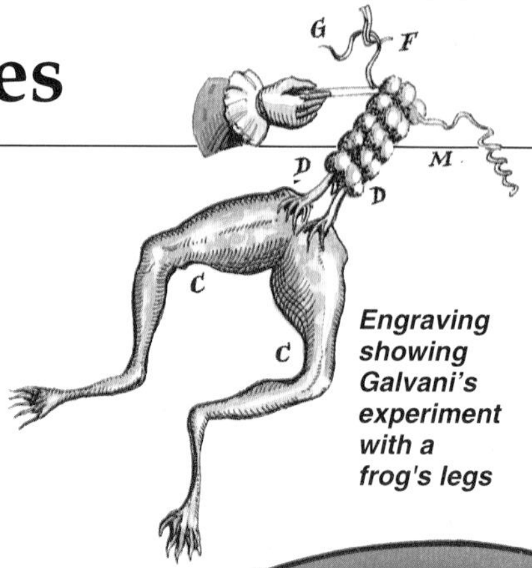

Engraving showing Galvani's experiment with a frog's legs

The first battery

Although people had known about the effects of natural electricity since ancient times, it took about 2000 years before anyone discovered how to harness it for their own ends.

The turning point came in 1794, when an Italian scientist called Alessandro Volta (1745-1827) built the first battery. He experimented with discs made of different metals, and finally made a pile from copper, cardboard and zinc. The cardboard was soaked in acid and sandwiched between the zinc and the copper. A chemical reaction between the substances transferred their chemical energy to electrical energy.

Sketch by Volta of his new invention

By providing a steady source of electricity for the first time ever, Volta's discovery supplied the key which made possible all future experiments with current electricity.

Supporting rods
Copper
Cardboard
Zinc
Wooden base

Volta's battery, known as a voltaic pile

Modern batteries

Modern cells and batteries are much more powerful and easier to use than Volta's pile. The most common one, used in hundreds of things, from alarm clocks to personal stereos, is called a dry cell. There are different kinds of dry cell, with slightly different ingredients. One of the most common ones contains zinc, a metal conductor and an electrolyte such as potassium hydroxide. Electrolytes are substances which contain charged particles called ions, or which release ions when dissolved. Electrolytes help the reaction between the other chemicals, because they help the charge carriers to move.

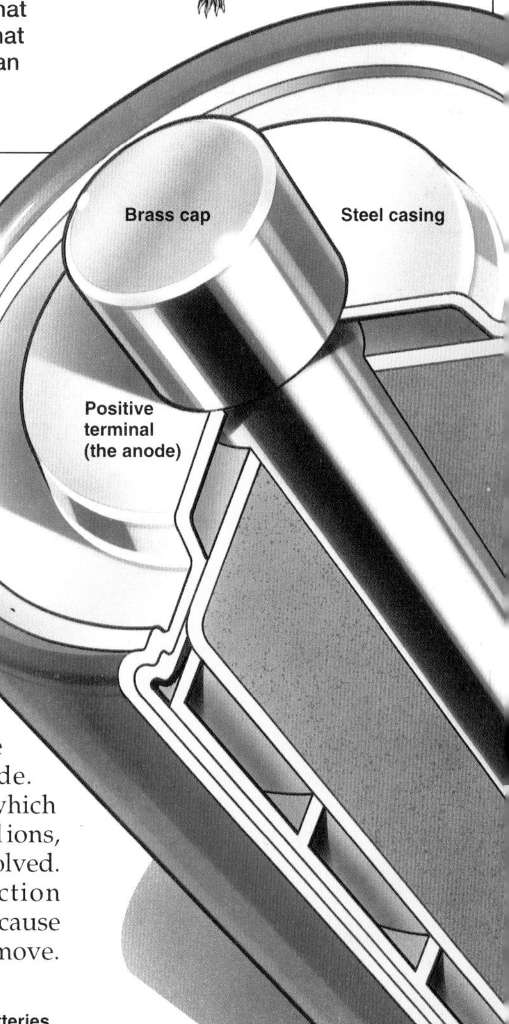

Brass cap
Steel casing
Positive terminal (the anode)

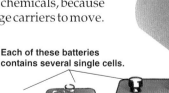

Single cells
Each of these batteries contains several single cells.

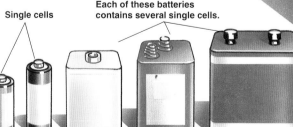

Make your own voltaic pile

You can make your own simple battery, using copper coins, kitchen foil (or zinc washers), paper towels, salty water and two pieces of insulated copper wire.

Find as many copper coins of the same size as you can. By drawing around one of the coins, cut out lots of discs from kitchen foil and paper towels. Soak the paper ones in a cup of very salty water. Then pile the discs in groups of three - foil, paper, copper - one on top of the other, until you have completed the pile. Each group of three discs makes one cell. The whole pile makes a battery.

Place the bare end of one piece of wire at the top of the pile, and the bare end of the other at the bottom. Then touch the two free ends together. If the room is very dark, you might even be lucky enough to see a spark.

You can use a pair of headphones to check whether your battery works. Wrap one bare wire around the bottom of the jackplug, and wrap the other around the middle. Attach paper clips to the other ends of each wire. Put on the headphones, then place one paper clip at the top and one at the bottom of the pile. Move the top paper clip around the disc. You should hear a crackle in your headphones. This is the electricity.

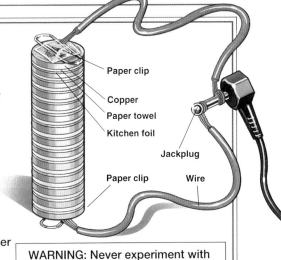

- Paper clip
- Copper
- Paper towel
- Kitchen foil
- Jackplug
- Paper clip
- Wire

WARNING: Never experiment with mains electricity. Don't attach your headphones to an ordinary battery or mains socket. It is extremely dangerous.

This dry cell has been cut open so you can see the insides.

- Cardboard/Metal outer casing
- Powdered zinc (negatively charged) and an alkaline electrolyte (usually potassium hydroxide)
- Metal conductor (positively charged)
- Manganese dioxide lining
- Negative terminal (the cathode)

Light cells

Although most cells are designed to transfer chemical energy into electricity, it is also possible to provide electricity from light energy. Cells which transfer light into electrical energy are called photovoltaic cells. They contain substances, such as silicon, called *semiconductors**.

Photovoltaic cells were first developed in the 1960s. They are found in pocket calculators, and on spacecraft and satellites. They are also used increasingly on a small-scale in hot countries, to provide electricity for purposes such as refrigeration.

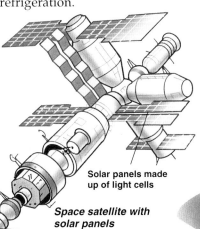

Solar panels made up of light cells

Space satellite with solar panels

The electric car

Cars have lots of electrical parts (the lights, for instance) which are powered by battery. Car batteries contain a number of special cells, called accumulators, that can accumulate, or build up, electrical energy as chemical energy. This energy can be released later, when it is needed.

Car battery Car batteries do not have to be replaced very often, because they are recharged by electricity transferred from the mechanical energy of the engine. Engineers are now designing accumulators that can store enough energy to power an entire vehicle.

Model of electrically powered car

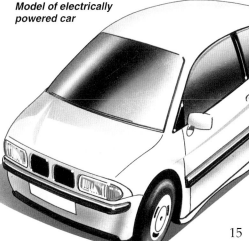

15

Electric circuits

Whenever you use electricity, whether it's by switching on a battery-powered cassette player, or using a computer plugged into the mains, you are completing a circuit. A circuit is a path for electricity, or electric current, that starts and finishes at the source of power. The power supply has two ends, called poles or terminals. Electricity flows between them by means of wires made of metal such as copper. Materials like these that can "carry" electricity are called conductors.

Although a current is often described as "flowing" through a circuit, it doesn't actually flow, because the effects are immediate. Current is also invisible. A wire looks and weighs the same whether or not it is carrying current. So the only way you can tell whether there is current in a circuit is by its effects. Circuits are designed for different purposes. The most familiar one is to produce heat or light, but circuits can be designed for chemical or magnetic effects too.

This is a simple circuit designed to light a small bulb. You can make one yourself with a few basic materials. Try increasing the voltage by adding a second and a third cell.

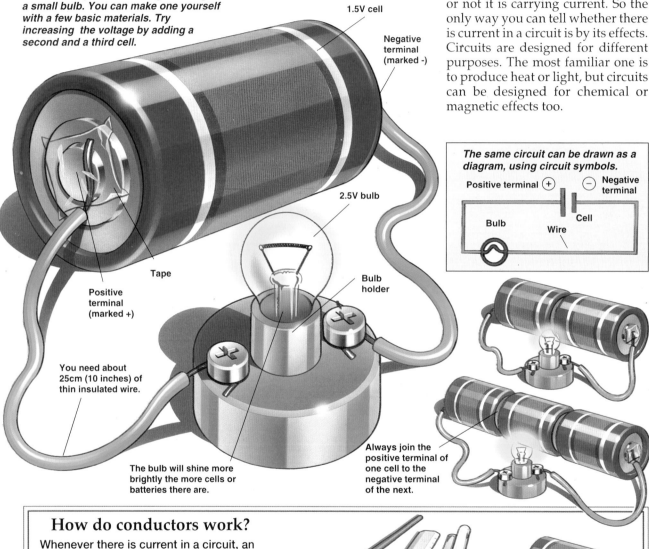

1.5V cell

Negative terminal (marked -)

2.5V bulb

Tape

Bulb holder

Positive terminal (marked +)

You need about 25cm (10 inches) of thin insulated wire.

The bulb will shine more brightly the more cells or batteries there are.

Always join the positive terminal of one cell to the negative terminal of the next.

The same circuit can be drawn as a diagram, using circuit symbols.

Positive terminal ⊕   ⊖ Negative terminal

Bulb   Cell

Wire

How do conductors work?

Whenever there is current in a circuit, an electrical charge is being carried through the circuit by electrons, the negatively charged parts of an atom. Good conductors (materials that carry electricity) are ones which contain "free", or "spare", electrons that can move easily.

To find out which materials make good conductors, you could try introducing different things into the circuit. See if the bulb still lights up.

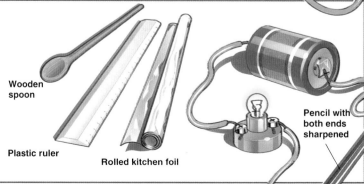

Wooden spoon

Plastic ruler

Rolled kitchen foil

Pencil with both ends sharpened

Measuring electricity

Current is measured in amperes, usually known as amps (A), named after the French scientist André-Marie Ampère. The number of amps an appliance needs varies a great deal. A calculator uses less than 1/100A (0.01A), while an electric heater may need about 10A.

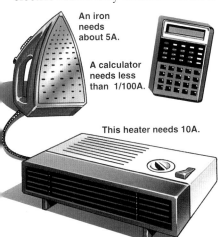

An iron needs about 5A.

A calculator needs less than 1/100A.

This heater needs 10A.

In order for current to flow in a circuit, it needs energy. Energy is measured in units called volts (V), named after Alessandro Volta (see page 14). The energy supplied to the circuit by the power source is called electromotive force (e.m.f.).

The number of volts, or voltage, required depends on the circuit. A bulb bright enough for a bicycle may only need a 3V battery, but a circuit with a kettle running off it will need a much higher voltage.

Insulation

Materials like rubber, plastic and wood have very few "free" electrons and so do not carry electricity. They

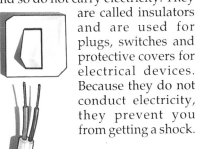

are called insulators and are used for plugs, switches and protective covers for electrical devices. Because they do not conduct electricity, they prevent you from getting a shock.

Electricity and chemistry

When an electric current flows through the wire in a circuit, no chemical change takes place. But just as the chemical energy in a cell or battery can be transferred to electrical energy, so electrical energy can sometimes be transferred to chemical energy. This process is called electrolysis.

Certain liquids, known as electrolytes, contain charged particles called ions. Positive ions are attracted to the negative terminal of an electricity supply (the cathode), and negative ions are attracted to the positive terminal (the anode). Electrolysis can be used to separate the positive ions of one

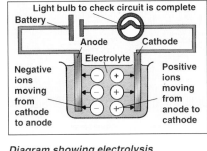

Diagram showing electrolysis

Light bulb to check circuit is complete
Battery
Anode   Cathode
Electrolyte
Negative ions moving from cathode to anode
Positive ions moving from anode to cathode

substance from the negative ions of another. For example, it is used to purify metals like sodium and potassium, which are only found in an impure form called an ore. It is also used for coating things in metal.

Copper plating

You can see the chemical effects of current by "plating" something in a thin layer of copper. You could try building a circuit like the one shown below. After a few minutes, carefully take the key out and rinse it gently in water. It should be thinly coated with a bright layer of copper.

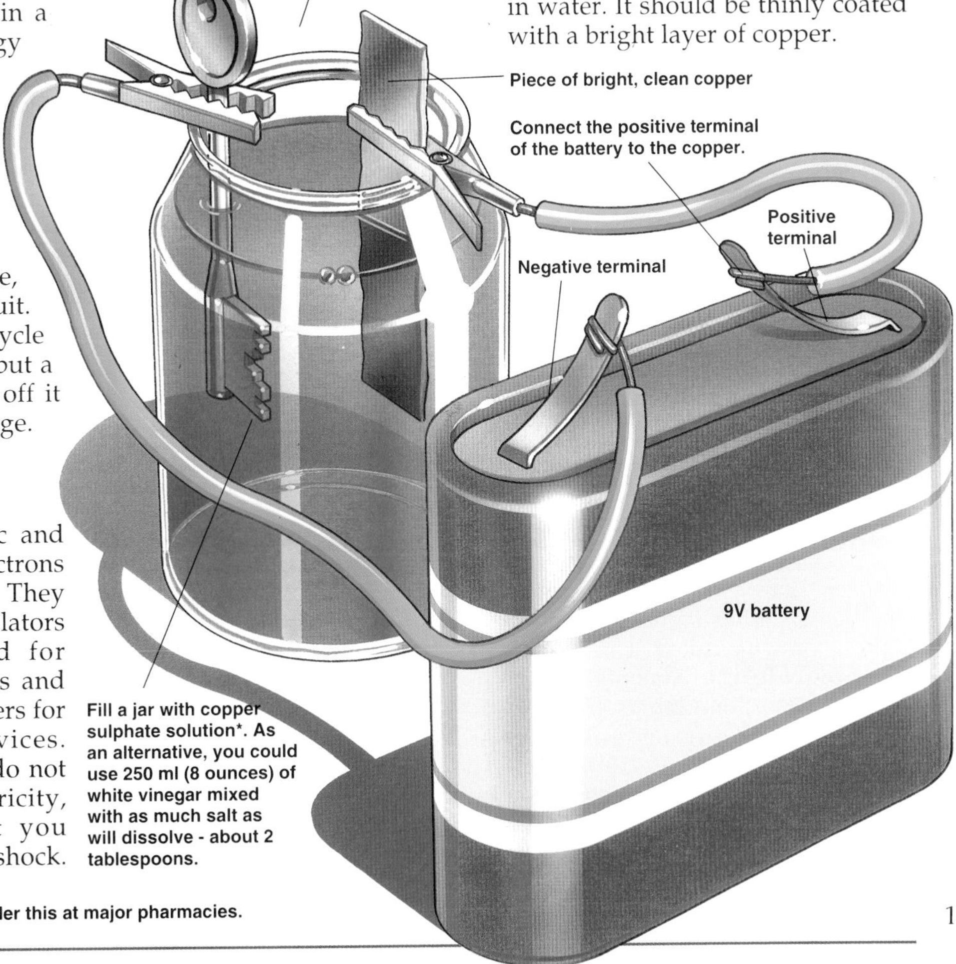

Connect the negative terminal to an old key.

The key and the copper should be close but not touching.

Piece of bright, clean copper

Connect the positive terminal of the battery to the copper.

Positive terminal

Negative terminal

9V battery

Fill a jar with copper sulphate solution*. As an alternative, you could use 250 ml (8 ounces) of white vinegar mixed with as much salt as will dissolve - about 2 tablespoons.

*You can buy or order this at major pharmacies.

Resistance: heat and light

Whenever current flows, some electrical energy is transferred to heat energy. The components in the circuit heat up, whether we want them to or not. This is caused by something called resistance - the ability of a substance to "resist", or oppose, the flow of an electric current. All electrical components have a certain resistance, even the wire which conducts the electricity. But the amount of heat produced depends on the size and type of materials used.

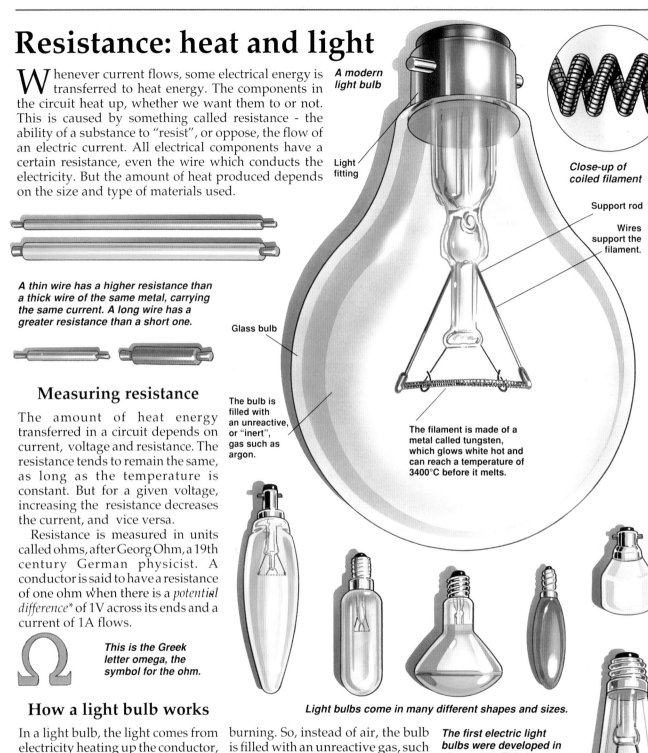

A modern light bulb

Light fitting

Close-up of coiled filament

Support rod

Wires support the filament.

Glass bulb

The bulb is filled with an unreactive, or "inert", gas such as argon.

The filament is made of a metal called tungsten, which glows white hot and can reach a temperature of 3400°C before it melts.

A thin wire has a higher resistance than a thick wire of the same metal, carrying the same current. A long wire has a greater resistance than a short one.

Measuring resistance

The amount of heat energy transferred in a circuit depends on current, voltage and resistance. The resistance tends to remain the same, as long as the temperature is constant. But for a given voltage, increasing the resistance decreases the current, and vice versa.

Resistance is measured in units called ohms, after Georg Ohm, a 19th century German physicist. A conductor is said to have a resistance of one ohm when there is a *potential difference** of 1V across its ends and a current of 1A flows.

This is the Greek letter omega, the symbol for the ohm.

How a light bulb works

In a light bulb, the light comes from electricity heating up the conductor, a piece of wire called a filament, inside the bulb. The filament is coiled to make room for a longer piece of wire. This creates greater resistance, which makes it glow white hot, giving off heat as well as light . Air contains oxygen, which would react with the hot filament to cause burning. So, instead of air, the bulb is filled with an unreactive gas, such as argon.

An electric fire is designed to give off heat and also has a high resistance, which causes it to glow. The filaments in an electric blanket have a lower resistance than the ones in a fire. They become warm without giving off any light.

Light bulbs come in many different shapes and sizes.

The first electric light bulbs were developed in about 1880. This is one designed by the American inventor Thomas Edison.

The filament was made of soot (carbonized slivers of bamboo).

The air was sucked out of the bulb to create a partial vacuum.

Did you know?

Air normally acts as an insulator, but if a voltage is high enough it can break down the resistance of the air around it to create sparks. Flash bulbs on cameras and spark plugs in cars make use of this by using high voltages to produce a spark. A lightning bolt is really just an enormous spark.

This shows an artificial lightning bolt of 1.3 million volts being used to test a power cable.

©Roger Ressmeyer, Starlight/Science Photo Library

Faulty circuits

Current always takes the shortest path between two terminals. If there is a weak point caused by a loose wire or damaged insulation, current may flow across it, instead of completing the circuit. This is called a short circuit. There may be a shower of sparks. If the voltage is very high, the circuit could get hot enough to start a fire.

You shouldn't use an appliance if you see sparks around it. A faulty circuit could allow current to flow through you, giving you a shock. If the voltage and current are high enough, the shock could kill you.

Series circuits

If you add another similar bulb to a simple circuit, like the one shown below, the resistance is doubled. This means that the energy available to each bulb is halved, making the light dimmer. The more bulbs you add, the dimmer the lights will be. If one of the lights breaks for some reason, the circuit is broken, and the other bulb goes out too. This kind of circuit is called a series circuit.

Parallel circuits

Household lights stay bright, even if you turn them all on at once. This is because they use a different kind of circuit, called a parallel circuit. A parallel circuit is made up of two or more separate circuits, sharing some of their conductors. In the parallel circuit below, the two bulbs are equally bright, but the battery will run out twice as fast as the one in the series circuit.

Simple series circuit

Battery

Bulb

Bulb

Wire

Simple parallel circuit

Battery

Wrap unprotected wire with masking tape.

Bulbs

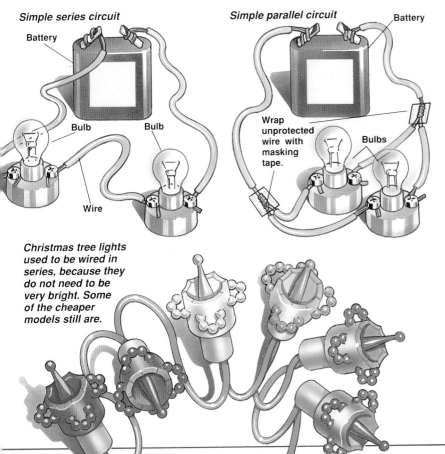

Christmas tree lights used to be wired in series, because they do not need to be very bright. Some of the cheaper models still are.

Make your own sparks

You can produce some very small, safe sparks by creating a fault in a simple circuit. Set up the experiment as shown below. Stroke one or two strands of wire with a piece of pencil lead.

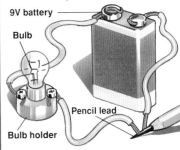

9V battery

Bulb

Pencil lead

Bulb holder

WARNING: Never experiment with mains electricity. It could kill you. Water can cause a short circuit, so you should never touch an appliance with wet hands.
  If you see someone receiving a shock, use a good insulator (something plastic or wooden) to push them away from the circuit. Turn it off immediately.

Electromagnetism

Electricity and magnetism can both attract things. But the difference is that magnets only attract certain materials, such as iron, while electrically charged objects can attract anything if it is very light. For centuries, scientists believed that there must be some sort of link, and puzzled over just what it was.

In 1820, a Danish scientist named Hans Christian Oersted stumbled upon a discovery that turned out to be very important. He found that when a current flowed through a wire it caused a nearby compass needle to change direction. When he changed the direction of the current, the compass needle changed direction too. The current in the wire did not seem to attract or repel the compass. Instead the needle settled at right angles to it.

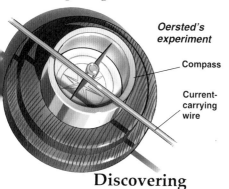

Oersted's experiment

Compass

Current-carrying wire

Discovering electromagnetism

Oersted's experiment was quickly repeated by others, including Ampère (see page 17), who found that an electric current produced a magnetic field around the wire it flowed through. This effect is called electromagnetism.

To see this for yourself, pierce a hole in a piece of thin cardboard and thread insulated wire through it. Fix the ends of the wire to the terminals of a battery and then sprinkle iron filings onto the cardboard.

Magnetic field lines

Ampère also discovered that the direction of the electromagnetic field depended on the direction of the current.

You can work this out using something called the "right-hand grip rule". Imagine holding a current-carrying wire with your fingers curled and your thumb pointing along it. Suppose the current flows (from positive to negative) in the direction of your thumb. Your curled fingers would then be pointing in the same direction as the lines of magnetic flux.

The first electromagnet

Ampère later came up with the idea that the magnetic field of a wire could be made much stronger if the wire was wound in a coil. Experiments proved he was right. When a current flows through a coil, the coil behaves like a bar magnet, and is called a solenoid.

In 1825, the English scientist William Sturgeon discovered that the magnetic strength of a solenoid could be enormously increased if a rod of soft iron was placed inside it. The rod is quickly magnetized and adds its own magnetic force to that of the solenoid. The combination of solenoid and core is called an electromagnet.

This diagram shows how an electromagnet is created using an iron bar and a solenoid.

Current flowing clockwise creates a south pole.

South pole

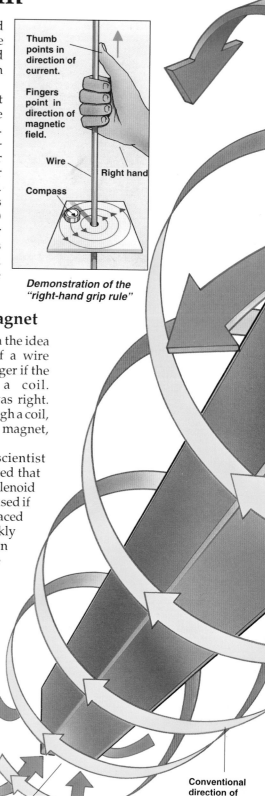

Thumb points in direction of current.

Fingers point in direction of magnetic field.

Wire

Right hand

Compass

Demonstration of the "right-hand grip rule"

Conventional direction of current flow

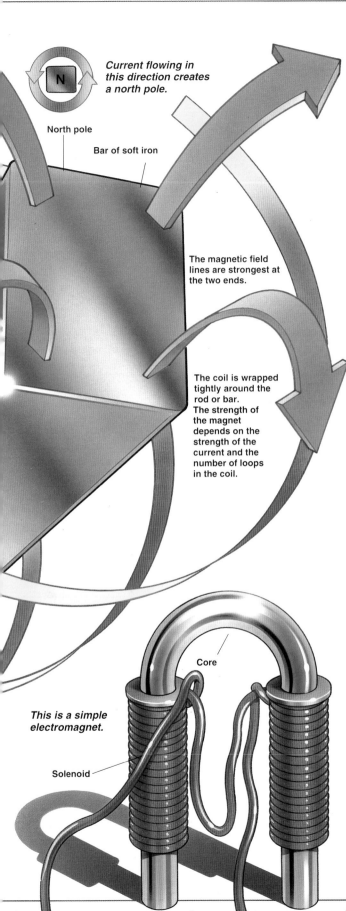

Current flowing in this direction creates a north pole.

North pole

Bar of soft iron

The magnetic field lines are strongest at the two ends.

The coil is wrapped tightly around the rod or bar. The strength of the magnet depends on the strength of the current and the number of loops in the coil.

This is a simple electromagnet.

Core

Solenoid

Make your own electromagnet

You can make your own electromagnet with a 4.5, 6 or 9V battery, an iron rod or nail and some insulated wire. To make a solenoid, wind the wire around a pencil as tightly as you can and link both ends to a battery with tape. It should be strong enough to affect a compass needle, but too weak to pick anything up . If you replace the pencil with the iron rod, you will have made an electromagnet that can pick up pins or paper clips.

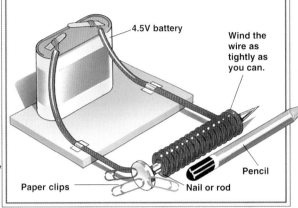

4.5V battery

Wind the wire as tightly as you can.

Paper clips

Nail or rod

Pencil

Switches, bells and buzzers

Electromagnets are used in electric switches, bells and buzzers. When an electromagnet is turned on, its magnetic field attracts any piece of iron or steel nearby. But it stops happening when it is turned off.

How an electric bell works

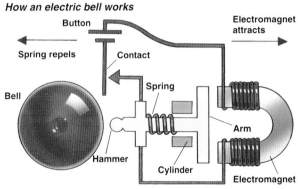

Button

Electromagnet attracts

Spring repels

Contact

Spring

Bell

Arm

Hammer

Cylinder

Electromagnet

When you press the button of an electric bell, current flows in the coils of an electromagnet, attracting a metal arm. As the arm moves nearer the electromagnet, it loses touch with the contact through which the current flows, so breaking the circuit. The arm is pulled back by the spring, causing the hammer to strike the bell. This completes the circuit and the cycle begins again. This constant switching on and off of the electromagnetic field is transferred to mechanical movement (the hammer hitting the bell) and sound (the bell ringing).

21

Using electromagnetism

Electromagnetism is the basis of all kinds of modern electrical devices - from tape recorders, microphones, loudspeakers and computers to electric motors and electromagnetic cranes.

How an electric guitar works

Inside the body of an electric guitar are magnetic "pick-ups", which have one magnet for each guitar string. The magnets are surrounded by a coil of wire, like a solenoid. Each magnet has its own magnetic field, which magnetizes the steel string immediately above it.

When you play the guitar, the strings vibrate and the movement disturbs the magnetic fields of the magnets in the pick-ups. This disturbance creates a small current in the coil. The current acts as an electrical signal, which is passed to an amplifier. The amplifier magnifies the signal so it can be used in a loudspeaker or a tape recorder.

For the clearest sound, the pick-ups should be still in relation to the strings. Electric guitars are made of solid wood. This stops them from passing on vibrations to the pick-ups.

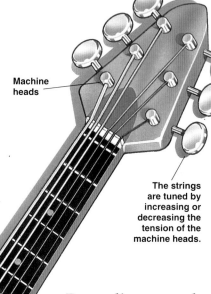

Machine heads

The strings are tuned by increasing or decreasing the tension of the machine heads.

Recording sounds

Sounds are really vibrations of air. In a cassette recorder, a microphone turns them into an electric current which varies according to the sound. The current flows through an electromagnet in the tape head to produce a fluctuating magnetic field.

Audio tape is covered with billions of needle-shaped iron or chromium oxide crystals that act like magnets. When tape passes the magnetic field of the tape head, the needles are moved into a pattern related to the sound coming into the microphone. When the machine is switched to "play", the tape passes the electromagnet of the head and induces a fluctuating current in it. This current then passes through an amplifier and on to a loudspeaker.

Close-up of magnetic pick-ups

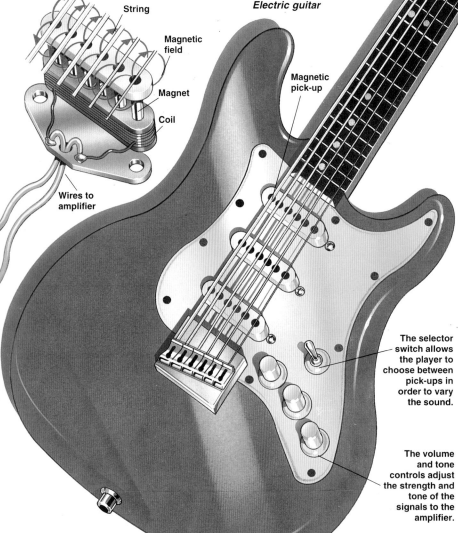

String

Magnetic field

Magnet

Coil

Wires to amplifier

Electric guitar

Magnetic pick-up

The selector switch allows the player to choose between pick-ups in order to vary the sound.

The volume and tone controls adjust the strength and tone of the signals to the amplifier.

Diagram showing tape head

Current

Coil

Head

Audio tape

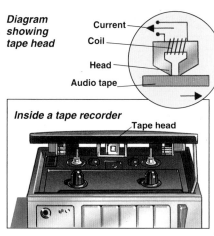

Inside a tape recorder

Tape head

How a loudspeaker works

Inside a loudspeaker, there is a permanent magnet and an electromagnetic coil attached to a cone called a diaphragm. Variations in current from a tape head, CD pick-up or record player stylus reach the loudspeaker after being amplified.

These variations affect the electromagnetic field of the coil. The attraction and repulsion between the coil's field and the field of the permanent magnet makes the coil and the diaphragm vibrate. The air in front of the diaphragm vibrates at the same speed and strength as the recorded sound or instrument.

Super electromagnets

Electromagnets can be made much more powerful in several ways: by increasing the current, by adding more loops to the coil and by putting the poles closer together. Cranes in steel works and scrap yards, where very heavy loads have to be lifted and moved, use extremely powerful electromagnets.

Some of the latest high-speed trains use electromagnets on the track and on the bottom of the train. The magnets repel each other, creating a magnetic field which lifts the train up and keeps it hovering about 10 centimetres (four inches) above the track. This reduces friction, allowing the train to move faster. The magnets are made of *superconducting** materials which reduce resistance to electricity.

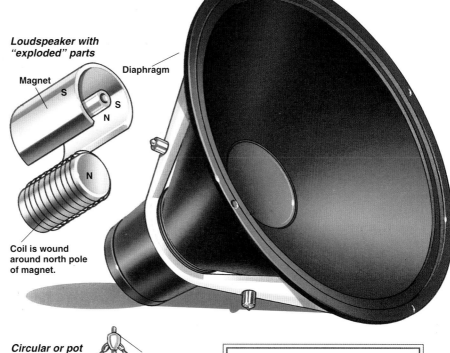

Loudspeaker with "exploded" parts

Magnet

Diaphragm

S
N
S
N

Coil is wound around north pole of magnet.

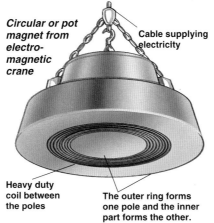

Circular or pot magnet from electro-magnetic crane

Cable supplying electricity

Heavy duty coil between the poles

The outer ring forms one pole and the inner part forms the other.

Cross-section of magnet

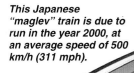

This Japanese "maglev" train is due to run in the year 2000, at an average speed of 500 km/h (311 mph).

Magnetize your voice

You can see the effect of magnetism on tape if you record something on a blank cassette. Then wind the tape back to the starting position and take it out of the machine. Unravel the tape and run a magnet over it several times. The magnet is unlikely to be powerful enough to erase the recording completely, but it will probably distort it. Feed the tape back into the cassette and play it back to find out what effect it has had.

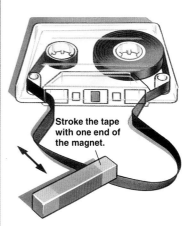

Stroke the tape with one end of the magnet.

Electric motors

Today almost any machine you can think of that is powered by electricity and has moving parts - from an electric drill to a washing machine - contains an electric motor.

The simplest way to understand how an electric motor works is to imagine a magnet free to spin around a single vertical rod or wire. If a second, fixed magnet is brought close, the swinging magnet will spin until the opposite poles are facing each other.

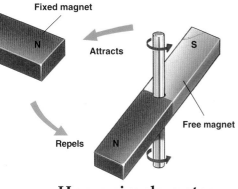

How a simple motor works

In an electric motor, instead of a "free" magnet, there is a coil of wire, called an armature, attached to a power supply. When current flows in the coil, it creates a magnetic field. Fixed magnets on each side of the coil provide fields which cause the coil to rotate. Current acts as if the charge carriers flow from positive to negative. The flow of current in the moving coil gives one side a north pole and the other a south pole. The armature spins until its poles are in line with the opposite poles of the fixed magnets.

Electric motors work because the flow of current in the armature is always changing direction. As the flow of current is reversed, the poles are reversed too. So as soon as the armature is facing one way, the contacts that carry the current from the power source switch positions. This is what keeps the armature rotating constantly.

Which way will the coil turn?

There is a simple way to calculate which way the coil will turn. It is called Fleming's Left Hand Rule. Hold out your left hand with your thumb, and first and second fingers at right angles to each other. Position your left hand so that the first finger points in the north-south direction of the magnetic field. The second finger will then be pointing in the direction of the current. The coil will turn in the direction in which the thumb is pointing.

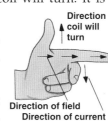

This modern electric motor has been "exploded" so you can see some of the parts inside.

Powerful motors

Instead of a coil linked to a pair of opposite pick-ups, commercial electric motors have many coils, each linked to a pair of opposite segments on a device called a commutator. This means that instead of receiving one push on each half turn, the multiple armature receives a series of pushes. The more coils there are, the smoother and more powerful the motor.

Simple electric motor
Fixed magnet
Rotating coil of armature
Fixed magnet
N
S
Contact
Battery

Coils carrying the current are wound around the armature.

Field coils

Soft iron armature with grooves for coils

Multi-slot commutator

The magnets are replaced with more powerful electromagnets. These are curved soft iron pole pieces shaped to fit closely around the armature and wound with coils to magnetize them.

Make your own electric motor

You can make a simple electric motor with a few basic materials. To build the armature, pierce a matchbox and cork with a metal rod (such as a knitting needle).

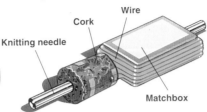

Knitting needle · **Cork** · **Wire** · **Matchbox**

Then wind a coil of insulated wire around the matchbox. Make as many loops as you can, and wind them tightly and neatly until you have covered the sides completely. Draw the ends along the cork and strip 2cm (1 inch) of insulation from each end. Bend the ends of the wire so that they slant away from the axis of the cork. Tape them to the cork opposite each other.

Now build a mount for the armature using a wooden board. Make holes for a split pin at each end of the board. Fix the pins high enough to allow the armature to spin freely when mounted on them.

To make brush contacts, fold two 6cm (2.5 inches) squares of kitchen foil until they are stiff enough to stand up firmly. Then cut two 25cm (10 inches) lengths of wire and strip away 2cm (1 inch) of insulation from the ends. Tuck one end of the length of wire into each "brush".

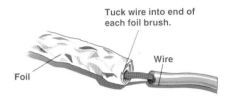

Tuck wire into end of each foil brush.

Foil · **Wire**

Bend the foil brushes and position them on the baseboard so that they will brush evenly against the wires on the cork. Then fix them to the board with tape. Rest the armature on its supporting pins, and adjust the brushes so they will not stop it from rotating. Fix a magnet on either side of the armature, so that a north-south field is created. Switch on the current by connecting the other ends of the wires to a 9V battery.

Did you know?

Scientists can now make tiny electric micromotors. Toshiba has developed one as small as 0.8mm (0.0315 of an inch) wide (shown here with a pen nib). Micromotors could be used in microsurgery and space research, and to circulate coolants in miniature circuits.

©Toshiba

The finished electric motor

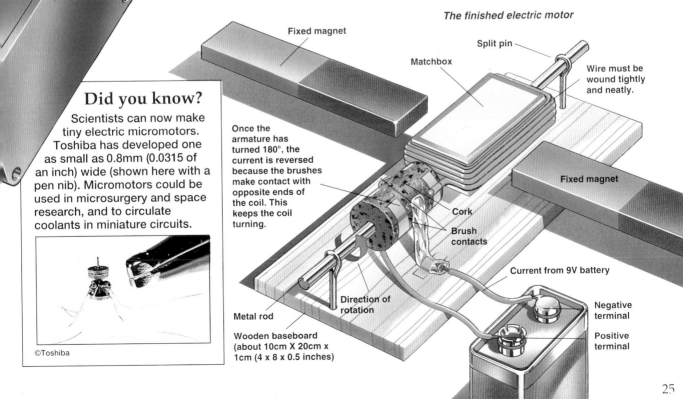

End shield · **Outer case** · **Terminal board**

Fixed magnet · **Split pin** · **Matchbox** · **Wire must be wound tightly and neatly.** · **Fixed magnet** · **Cork** · **Brush contacts** · **Current from 9V battery** · **Negative terminal** · **Positive terminal**

Once the armature has turned 180°, the current is reversed because the brushes make contact with opposite ends of the coil. This keeps the coil turning.

Direction of rotation · **Metal rod** · **Wooden baseboard (about 10cm X 20cm x 1cm (4 x 8 x 0.5 inches)**

Generating electricity

Most of the electricity we use is produced, or "generated", in power stations, using huge machines called generators. Today we take for granted the existence of an electricity supply, but it is less than 200 years since the first generator was invented.

After the amazing revelation that electricity could produce magnetism (see page 20), scientists began wondering whether magnetism could also be used to generate, or "induce", electricity. Finally, in 1831, the English scientist Michael Faraday made an important breakthrough. He wound two lengths of insulated wire in coils around opposite sides of a soft iron ring. The first coil was connected to a voltaic pile. The ends of the second coil were connected by a copper wire passing over a magnetic needle.

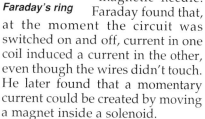

Faraday's ring

Faraday found that, at the moment the circuit was switched on and off, current in one coil induced a current in the other, even though the wires didn't touch. He later found that a momentary current could be created by moving a magnet inside a solenoid.

The next step was to look for a way to induce a continuous current. Faraday achieved this by spinning a copper disc through the narrow gap of a strong horseshoe magnet.

But he soon discovered that a more efficient method was to rotate a coil of wire between the opposite poles of a magnet. He had found the principle behind all modern generators - from a simple dynamo on a bicycle to the type of generator used in a power station.

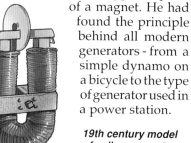

19th century model of a disc generator

What drives the generator?

In order to drive a generator, energy is needed. In most power stations this is supplied as heat from burning fuels, or from nuclear energy. But generators can be powered by all kinds of energy.

A bicycle light can be powered by a dynamo, which transfers mechanical energy from your legs pushing the pedals. Modern windmills, or wind turbines, generate electricity from the wind (the energy of moving air). Fast-moving water from a river, or falling from a dammed lake, can also be used to turn a water-wheel or drive a turbine, which can then turn a generator.

© John Mead/Science Photo Library

A dammed lake for storing water at a hydroelectric power station

Inside a power station

In power stations that burn fossil fuels, there are four main steps involved in generating electricity. These are shown below.

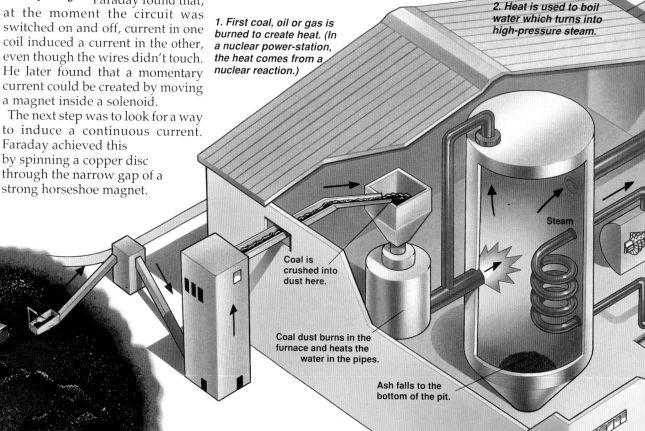

1. First coal, oil or gas is burned to create heat. (In a nuclear power-station, the heat comes from a nuclear reaction.)

2. Heat is used to boil water which turns into high-pressure steam.

Steam

Coal is crushed into dust here.

Coal dust burns in the furnace and heats the water in the pipes.

Ash falls to the bottom of the pit.

Inside a bicycle dynamo

A bicycle dynamo (shown here) is rather like an electric motor working backwards. Inside is a coil wound on a soft iron core and mounted on an axle. The coil spins when the axle head is in contact with the bicycle wheel. On the outside of the coil are two fixed magnets. The movement of the coil across the lines of the field induces a current.

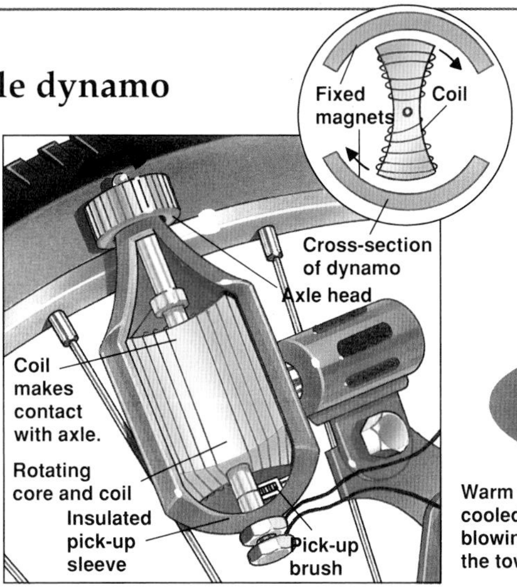

Fixed magnets

Coil

Cross-section of dynamo

Axle head

Coil makes contact with axle.

Rotating core and coil

Insulated pick-up sleeve

Pick-up brush

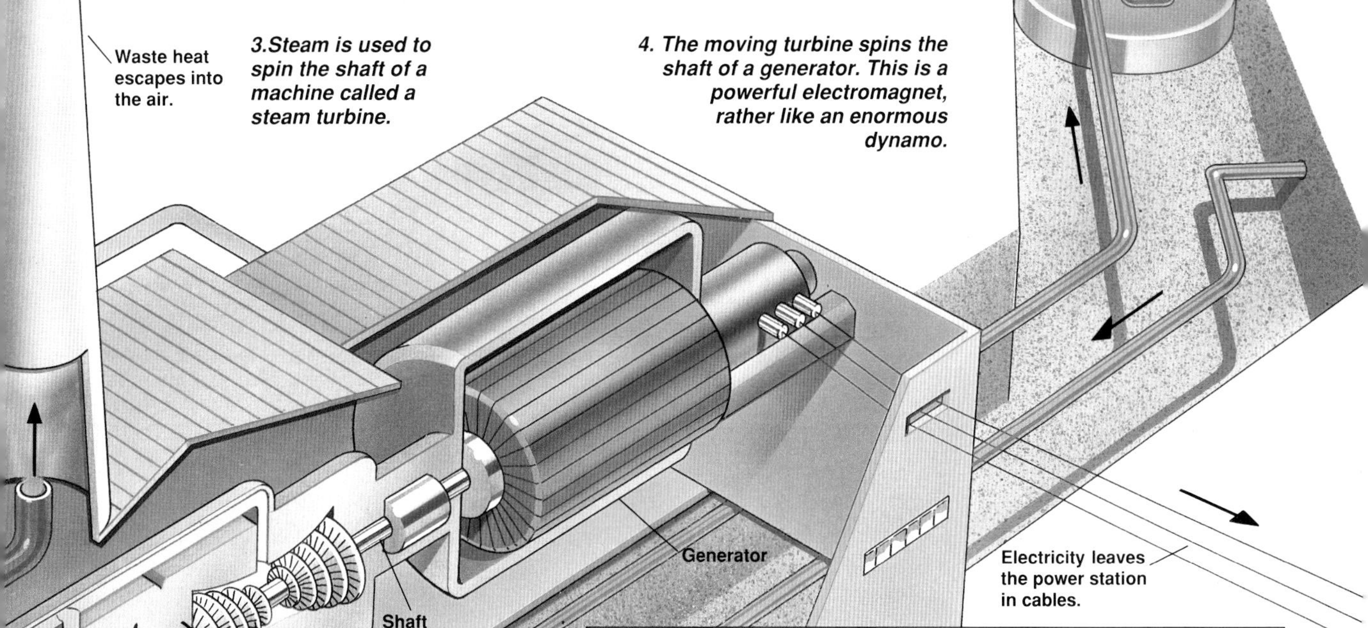

Warm water is cooled by air blowing through the tower.

Waste heat escapes into the air.

3. Steam is used to spin the shaft of a machine called a steam turbine.

4. The moving turbine spins the shaft of a generator. This is a powerful electromagnet, rather like an enormous dynamo.

Generator

Electricity leaves the power station in cables.

Shaft

Steam turbine

Warm water

Cool water from river or sea.

How generators work

The electricity supplied by a battery flows in one direction and is called direct current (d.c.). The current supplied by a power station is called alternating current (a.c.), because it is constantly changing direction. An a.c. generator works rather like an electric motor in reverse. Like electric motors, the generators have coils. Turning the coil between two magnets induces a current, which changes direction every half-turn.

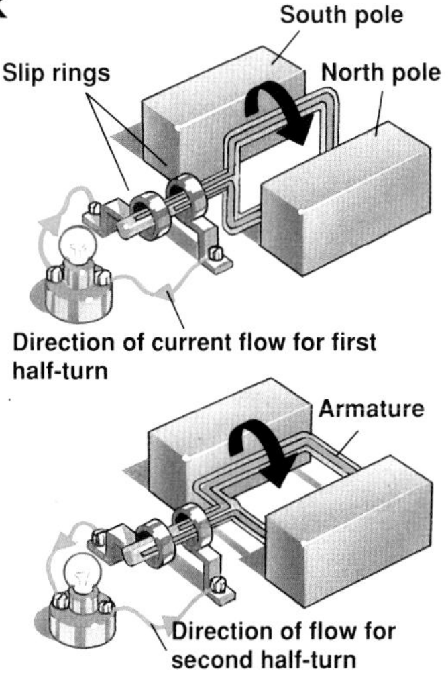

Slip rings

South pole

North pole

Direction of current flow for first half-turn

Armature

Direction of flow for second half-turn

27

Electricity at home

Electricity is transmitted around the country in a network of cables called a grid system. But, like all conductors, cables offer resistance, and transfer some of the electrical energy to other forms such as heat. This heating effect rises with the size of the current. But it can be reduced by decreasing the current and increasing the voltage. This is done by devices called "step-up" transformers.

Before the electricity can be used in people's homes, the voltage has to be decreased and the current increased. This is done by "step down" transformers at the other end.

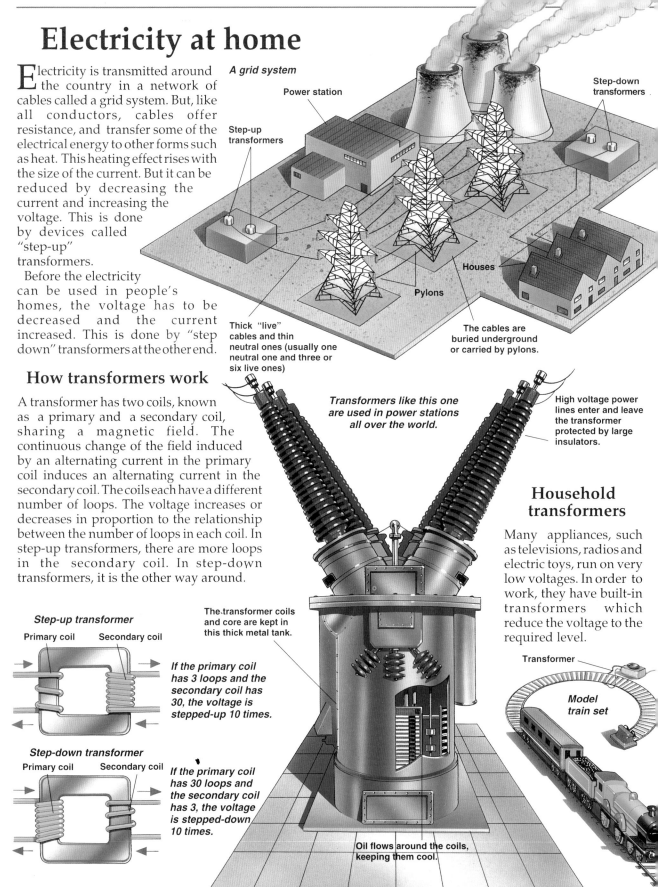

A grid system

Power station

Step-up transformers

Step-down transformers

Houses

Pylons

Thick "live" cables and thin neutral ones (usually one neutral one and three or six live ones)

The cables are buried underground or carried by pylons.

How transformers work

A transformer has two coils, known as a primary and a secondary coil, sharing a magnetic field. The continuous change of the field induced by an alternating current in the primary coil induces an alternating current in the secondary coil. The coils each have a different number of loops. The voltage increases or decreases in proportion to the relationship between the number of loops in each coil. In step-up transformers, there are more loops in the secondary coil. In step-down transformers, it is the other way around.

Transformers like this one are used in power stations all over the world.

High voltage power lines enter and leave the transformer protected by large insulators.

Household transformers

Many appliances, such as televisions, radios and electric toys, run on very low voltages. In order to work, they have built-in transformers which reduce the voltage to the required level.

Step-up transformer

Primary coil   Secondary coil

The transformer coils and core are kept in this thick metal tank.

If the primary coil has 3 loops and the secondary coil has 30, the voltage is stepped-up 10 times.

Step-down transformer

Primary coil   Secondary coil

If the primary coil has 30 loops and the secondary coil has 3, the voltage is stepped-down 10 times.

Oil flows around the coils, keeping them cool.

Transformer

Model train set

Bringing the power home

The electricity cable enters your house via a safety device called a fuse (see below). The current then flows through a meter, which works rather like a very simple electric motor. It has a disc which rotates faster as more current flows. As it spins, it pushes around numbers on a dial, showing how much electricity has been supplied.

At the fuse-box, the wires divide into parallel circuits that carry the electricity around different parts of the house. There are three types of circuit: ring mains circuits (for the sockets), lighting circuits and the circuit for cooking.

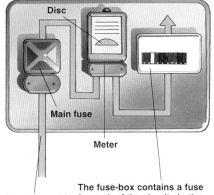

Disc

Main fuse

Meter

Incoming cable containing a live wire and a neutral wire

The fuse-box contains a fuse for each of the circuits in the house. If too much current flows, the fuse pops out and the circuit is broken.

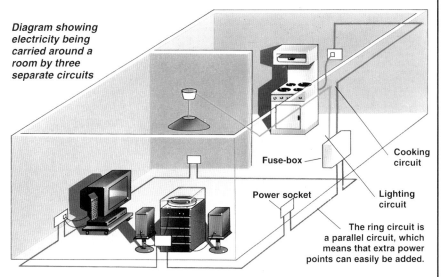

Diagram showing electricity being carried around a room by three separate circuits

Fuse-box

Cooking circuit

Power socket

Lighting circuit

The ring circuit is a parallel circuit, which means that extra power points can easily be added.

How fuses work

Fuses are electrical safety devices, found in fuse-boxes and plugs, which work by stopping the flow of current if a fault develops. They are made of wire that conducts electricity well, but has a low melting point. Too much current makes the wire so hot that it melts, breaking the circuit. When this happens, the fuse is said to have "blown". It is important not to replace the fuse until the fault in the circuit has been mended.

Fuses are labelled in amps, according to the amount of current they will carry before melting (for a given voltage). For example, a 13A fuse contains thicker wire and will offer less resistance than a 3A fuse. It is dangerous to use a fuse with a higher rating than the circuit requires. It may allow too much current to flow, which could permanently damage the appliance.

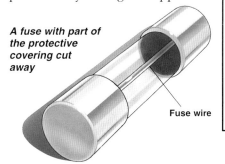

A fuse with part of the protective covering cut away

Fuse wire

Plugs and switches

Plugs connect electrical appliances to the ring main. Each plug contains a live and a neutral wire. When a plug is put into a socket, the pins connect with live and neutral points behind the socket. This forms a circuit, linking the appliance with the electricity supply.

For safety reasons, most plugs contain a fuse, as well as some form of "earthing" system. Many two-pin plugs have a metal earthing strip on the outside. Three-pin plugs have an earth pin. If an appliance is faulty, current will flow through the pin, rather than through the person using it. Most sockets also have a switch. When the switch is off, electricity will not flow in the appliance, even if it is plugged in.

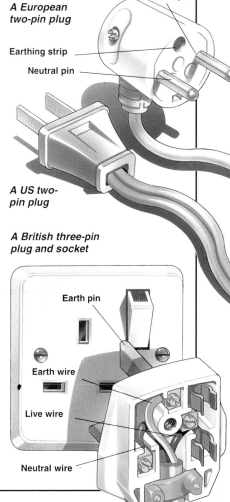

A European two-pin plug

Live pin

Earthing strip

Neutral pin

A US two-pin plug

A British three-pin plug and socket

Earth pin

Earth wire

Live wire

Neutral wire

Electricity in the future

A hundred years ago, it would have been hard to imagine the extraordinary developments in technology that were about to take place. Although we can can only guess at the changes the next century will bring, it is still possible to make some reasonable predictions.

The electronic age

Some of the most likely advances related to electricity and magnetism will be in electronics and computer systems. Many cities today are dominated by huge office blocks and traffic jams, as thousands travel to work. But this may change as more and more people are able to work, shop and even attend school, via a VDU screen at home.

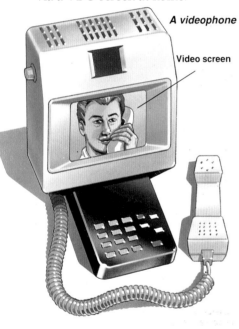

A videophone

Video screen

By using videophones, executives will be able to "attend" meetings without having to travel to them. Contracts will be signed thousands of miles away, using "light pens" at a video terminal. Shopping may be done from home too, with the help of television links between shops, warehouses and the home. Cash will gradually fall out of use, as electronic debit cards, linked directly to a bank account, become more common.

Speech recognition

It is already possible for some computers to interpret sound patterns and recognize voices. In the future, you will probably be able to unlock your front door and car with a password that a security computer can recognize. You may also be able to turn on the television or boil a kettle with only a spoken command.

Medicine

Computers will be used to compare data and computer diagnosis will become routine. This will help doctors to detect susceptibility to an illness and take steps to prevent it. Magnetic scanning machines, which allow a doctor to see inside a body, without the use of potentially harmful x-rays, will be widespread. These work by translating variations in magnetic fields in a person's body to a simulated image on a screen.

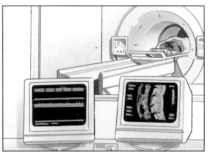

Magnetic scanner in use

Satellite surveillance

Satellites will be linked electronically to a global network of information banks. Atmospheric surveillance will enable computers to forecast the weather and to give advance warning of storms, floods and hurricanes, as well as dangerously high levels of pollution. Satellite ground surveillance will help farmers to increase harvests and to protect crops from disease. Electronic listening devices will record the movement of groups of fish, enabling us to prevent overfishing.

© Nasa/Science Photo Library

Satellite image showing ozone depletion over the Antarctic

Robots

Robots are already used in dangerous environments (for example, inside a nuclear reactor), and for carrying out precise and repetitive tasks (like welding car bodies on assembly lines). They are likely to become much more sophisticated, with a range of mechanical limbs and electronic sensors to detect light, sound, temperature and pressure. As electrical circuits and microchips are increasingly miniaturized, more complex robots will be built, capable of designing and building even more complex robots themselves.

Industrial robot used inside nuclear reactor

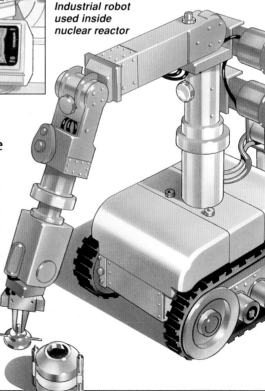

Alternative energy sources

Concern about pollution and the possibility of exhausting the earth's supply of fossil fuels means that there will be increasing dependence on "renewable" energy sources. Many of these are already in use on a small-scale, but further advances will enable them to be more widely used.

Many power stations already run on hydroelectric power, which uses fast flowing water to spin turbines. Rivers are dammed to store water, which is then released at high speed. But mechanical energy from the movement of waves may be used increasingly in tidal barrages and wave power generators.

Diagram of wave power generator

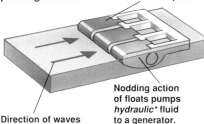

Floats on concrete spine

Nodding action of floats pumps *hydraulic** fluid to a generator.

Direction of waves

Geothermal energy is already being used to generate electricity. Sources include natural heat deep in the Earth, steam from geysers and the exploitation of heat differentials. Scientists are now researching the use of differences in temperature between deep water and water near the surface, in a technique known as Ocean Thermal Energy Conversion.

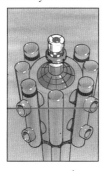

OTEC machine

Solar panels, made up of photovoltaic cells, use light energy from the Sun to generate electricity. Solar technology is not yet organized for general use, but it is used increasingly in hot countries, for specific purposes, such as providing irrigation pumping systems or refrigeration.

Glossary

Here is a list explaining some of the most common words associated with electricity and magnetism, as well as some other unfamiliar terms used in the book. When a word appears in *italic* type, it has its own entry in the list.

Alternating current (a.c.). A continuous electric *current* that constantly changes direction. The type of current supplied by a power station.

Ampere. The unit of measurement of electric *current*.

Angle of declination. The difference beween magnetic north and "true north". This angle varies from place to place around the world.

Anode. The positive terminal of an electrical *circuit*.

Atom. The name given to the smallest particles that make up an element, and can take part in a chemical reaction. Atoms were once thought to be indivisible, but scientists now know that they are made up of many smaller units or particles.

Battery. A source of electrical energy made up of more than one *electrical cell*.

Cathode. The negative terminal of an electrical *circuit*.

Circuit. A continuous path for electric *current* that begins and ends at the source of power. A circuit is made up of a number of *conductors*.

Conductor. A material, such as copper wire, through which electricity can flow relatively easily.

Current. A flow of electric *charge* through a *conductor*, such as a metal.

Direct current (d.c.). A continuous electric current that flows in one direction only. *Batteries* supply direct current.

Dynamo. The name given to a small generator (for example, on a bicycle) for transferring mechanical *energy* to electrical energy.

Electric charge. A property of some elementary particles which causes them to exert forces on each other.

Electrical cell. A device which produces an electric *current* by means of a chemical reaction. A single cell is made up of a pair of substances. Several cells make up a *battery*.

Electrolysis. The breakdown of chemicals using electric *current*.

Electrolyte. A substance which releases *ions* when dissolved.

Electromotive force (e.m.f.). The *energy* supplied to a *circuit* by the power source.

Electron. A negatively charged particle or unit in an *atom*.

Energy. The capacity of anything to move or change.

Fossil fuel. A naturally occuring fuel, such as coal, petroleum or natural gas, formed by the fossilization of prehistoric organisms.

Insulator. A material such as plastic or wood that does not allow electricity to flow through it. Used in plugs and switches and protective covers for electrical appliances.

Ion. An *atom* or group of atoms with an unequal number of *protons* and *electrons*. Positive ions have more protons than electrons. Negative ions have more electrons than protons.

Ionize. To produce *ions*. This can be as a result of a chemical reaction, discharge of electricity, dissolving an *electrolyte* or ionizing radiation.

Joule. The unit used in the measurement of *energy*. One joule is the amount of energy suplied when the temperature of one kilogram of water rises by 1°C.

Latitude. Distance in degrees north or south of the equator.

Nucleus. The central part of an *atom*, made up of *protons* and *neutrons*.

Neutralize. To make electrically neutral by balancing a positive or negative *charge* with an opposite charge of equal strength.

Neutron. An uncharged unit or particle in the *nucleus* of an *atom*.

Nuclear power. Electrical *energy* generated by nuclear fission - splitting the *nuclei* of unstable or relatively large radioactive *atoms*.

Ohm. The unit of measurement of *electrical resistance*.

Potential. A measure of the work needed to move an electrically charged object in an electric field.

Potential difference. The difference in *energy* between two points in an electric *circuit*.

Proton. A positive unit or particle in the *nucleus* of an *atom*.

Resistance. The ability of a substance to resist, or oppose, the flow of an electric *current*. Measured in units called *ohms*.

Semiconductor. A substance between an *insulator* and a *conductor*, whose electrical conductivity rises with temperature.

Superconductor. A substance that has no electrical *resistance*. In metals this occurs at very low temperatures, but in certain ceramic materials it can occur at higher temperatures.

Volt. A unit of electrical *potential energy*.

Watt. The unit of measurement of power - the rate of doing work.

Index

The publishers would like to thank Brook Crompton and Siemens plc for the loan of material on electric motors to use as artist's reference.